THE SECRET DIARY
OF PRINCE CHARLES
AGED 47¾

Philip Honour

MINERVA PRESS

LONDON

MONTREUX   LOS ANGELES   SYDNEY

THE SECRET DIARY OF PRINCE CHARLES AGED 47¾
Copyright © Philip Honour 1997

All Rights Reserved

ISBN 1 86106 627 9

First Published 1997 by
MINERVA PRESS
195 Knightsbridge
London SW7 1RE

Printed in Great Britain for Minerva Press

THE SECRET DIARY
OF PRINCE CHARLES
AGED 47¾

*Thanks to Christine Honour,
David Hughes and Gary Vincent.*

Monday 1st January

Another new year and I'm still unemployed. I wonder if this is the year when I will get the job. I've only two New Year's resolutions to make this year, and they are:

1. To become king.
2. To keep out of the newspapers as much as possible.

I suppose if I achieve one of the above it will be better than I've ever done before.

Tuesday 2nd January

Still no hints from Mother as to whether I will get the job this year. I keep hoping that today will be the day she decides to retire. It irritates me that she never refers to me as Charles but always calls me Prince. Does she think I'm a naffing Alsatian?

Wednesday 3rd January

I'm convinced I would make an excellent king. When Mother is out, I've practised wearing the crown and I can now balance it on my ears so that it doesn't slip down over my eyes.

Thursday 4th January

Since I was a toddler I've always felt that one day I would be the most important person in the country. In fact, ever since I was just twelve inches tall, I felt I was big enough to be a ruler.

6

Friday 5th January

I've tried dropping Mother a few hints lately but I don't know if she will get the message. Today I left an application form for an old age pensioner bus pass on her desk. I think she worries about how she will live on an old age pension, especially as Father has been out of work for so long.

Saturday 6th January

Another depressing day today. The day started all right with breakfast in bed at 11 a.m. Eggy soldiers today... my favourite. After that though, things just went from bad to worse. First Diana phoned begging for money for a new dress. I only had £10,000 in the house to give her so she now thinks I'm mean. This afternoon, Norris McWhirter from *The Guinness Book of Records* phoned saying he wanted to include me in next year's book because I am serving the longest ever recorded apprenticeship.

Sunday 7th January

Had an appointment at the royal hairdresser's today. He said it probably wouldn't need cutting again for at least a couple of months. That seems odd as I used to have a haircut every month. He said if I came every month he would only be able to give me a polish.

Monday 8th January

William and Harry came to visit me today (on their own thank goodness). William laughed at my haircut saying that he would now be heir to the throne and that I am hairless to the throne. I'm afraid I didn't see the funny side and confiscated his new rugby ball as a punishment.

Tuesday 9th January

Today Aunt Margaret visited which put the whole household in a panic. Ever since the Windsor fire, Mother has a dread of visitors who smoke coming into the house. It seems everywhere you turn there is an ash tray and a fire extinguisher.

Wednesday 10th January

Yesterday's visit passed without incident, but the dread of Aunt Margaret's smoking affects Mother's nerves badly. She is convinced she will start another fire. I'm sure I glimpsed Mother outside having a crafty cigarette to calm her nerves.

Thursday 11th January

The last few days have been extremely stressful and today I woke up with an awful toothache. I have found that smoke always starts it off. I am one of the privileged and can still claim dental treatment on the National Health Service. I phoned the dentist but he can't see me until Monday. (I hope I survive that long).

Friday 12th January

Wretched tooth still hurting so phoned dentist again. His receptionist said he couldn't possibly see me today because he's due on the first tee at 9 a.m. I must remember to tell Mother not to include him on the list for OBEs for the next few years, although he may get my vote for sports personality of the year.

Saturday 13th January

If it wasn't for my toothache, I'd probably enjoy the weekend. I look forward to not having to go to the job centre. William and Harry visited today and they could hardly contain their excitement when I offered to take them on a tour of the local architecture. Unfortunately, they had to cancel at the last minute because of a prior engagement. I suppose it must have been really important.

Sunday 14th January

I'm really dreading tomorrow. There are two places where I really hate going. The first is the Royal Variety Performance and the other is the dentist. At least the dentist's visit will be over in a few minutes. Sometimes the Royal Variety Performance seems to last weeks.

Monday 15th January

It's funny the things that cross your mind when you're sat in the dreaded dentist's chair. Whilst the dentist was probing and drilling I tried to imagine I was at my coronation. I usually find this takes my mind off things. Then I heard, "I think I'll have to give you a crown." Unfortunately it was the voice of the dentist I heard and not Mother's.

Tuesday 16th January

I think when I become king, I will bring the monarchy into the twenty-first century and I will follow the example of the youth of today. I've never liked the sound of King Charles so instead I'll be known as symbol, the monarch formerly known as Prince.

Wednesday 17th January

Mother seems to have been suffering some discomfort recently. She seems to find it difficult to remain seated for any length of time. Still it has given me the opportunity to try out the throne for size. I've also seen Edward sitting there once or twice dressed in all the ceremonial robes. I'm not sure if he has ideas above his station or if he is just rehearsing for his latest play. I think I'll have to watch him just in case.

Thursday 18th January

I had a terrible night last night. At about 2 a.m. I was woken up by the wailing of sirens. I didn't bother to get up to investigate as I assumed it was yet another unwanted intruder who had got into Mother's bedroom. It took me ages to get back to sleep but I managed to in the end, in the usual way, by counting foxes.

Friday 19th January

After being disturbed during the night, I overslept this morning not waking up until lunch time. Obviously I was in a terrible mood by then because Mother had not brought me my breakfast in bed, so I stormed into her room to complain but she wasn't there. In fact there was nobody in the whole palace apart from the two hundred and fifty servants of course. I decided there was only one course of action to take so I went straight back to bed and awaited the family's return.

Saturday 20th January

It turned out the sirens I heard were not due to an intruder as I suspected, rather it was an ambulance rushing Mother to hospital. I think she could have waited until morning, after she had got my breakfast. By bedtime I was feeling weak with hunger as I had spent all day trying to find the kitchen, a room I had never needed to find before. How simple life must be for ordinary people with only half a dozen rooms.

Sunday 21st January

I phoned the hospital today to find out how Mother was. I actually managed to speak to a doctor who said she was suffering from a severe case of haemorrhoids and that it was yet another 'anus horriblis' for her.

Monday 22nd January

The doctor at the hospital decided that Mother should stay there for a few days until she has fully recovered. Unfortunately Father has decided to take charge of catering at home. So far he has arranged to have meals delivered to us from a Greek takeaway. To really make him feel at home, he insists on us eating to the accompaniment of his Nana Mouskouri records. If the food doesn't make me throw up, the music certainly will.

Tuesday 23rd January

Today Mother summoned me to her hospital bedside. She said she felt I would now be able to handle some of her important tasks whilst she was incapacitated. She handed me a list:

1. Pay the milkman
2. Collect her pension from the post office
3. Feed the corgis.

I feel so proud at being entrusted with such awesome responsibilities.

Wednesday 24th January

I managed to pay the milkman without any problems but collecting the pension at the post office proved a more tricky assignment. I was given preferential treatment, or so I was told, only having to queue for half an hour. I was then asked for identification. We royals usually have no need for wallets and things like that, so I had no documents or credit cards with me. However, I think that two hours in the tower convinced the cashier that I was who I said I was – and he paid up.

Thursday 25th January

I visited Mother in hospital again today. She was in a very distressed state. It seems the previous evening she was visited by Diana who was doing one of her regular rounds, visiting patients. The doctor in charge seems to think this will probably set back her recovery by at least a month.

Friday 26th January

Apart from the catering things seem to be running pretty smoothly at home and I seem to have justified the faith that Mother has in me. The country seems blissfully unaware that the Queen is not carrying out her normal duties. I am a bit concerned though that a couple of the dogs seem a bit off colour.

Saturday 27th January

Popped in to see Mother again today. She seemed a lot better until I broke the news that two of the corgis had died. She asked how many times a day I had been feeding them. I had only fed them once this week as per her instructions as I thought that was sufficient. I left the hospital with my tail between my legs – something those pooches would never do again.

Sunday 28th January

Mother has decided to discharge herself from hospital and she will be coming back home tomorrow. She decided the chance of Diana visiting again was not one she was prepared to take. I must say I am delighted with her decision as I don't think I could face another Greek takeaway.

Monday 29th January

Things are nearly back to normal. Mother is back home and the only sign that she is not quite herself is the rather large cushion which is now positioned on the throne. She has now resumed her normal duties so it's back to the job centre for me.

Tuesday 30th January

I phoned the job centre today to see if there was anything available, but once they knew my age and experience I knew I had no chance. I tried to talk over my situation with Father but with his limited work experience and the fact he doesn't speak much English, I didn't get very far. It didn't help matters that it was his interpreter's day off.

Wednesday 31st January

I still feel rather guilty about the death of two of Mother's corgis and I know she is still upset. It is quite sad to see her out walking in the garden dragging two empty leads behind her. I think I will try to get her a couple of replacements.

Thursday 1st February

It seems to be rather difficult to get corgis as Mother only wants pedigree ones. I've tried several pet shops but everybody seems to want to sell me King Charles spaniels. I seem to recall we had the same problem when trying to buy a stereo system last year. Everybody wanted to sell us a Phillips or a Ferguson.

Friday 2nd February

I have decided the best thing to do is to try to breed some puppies using one of Mother's bitches and finding a breeder with a suitable pedigree dog. As luck would have it there was a suitable advertisement in today's paper. The chap is coming round to the house on Monday to carry out the service.

Saturday 3rd February

Today was a day of great celebrations. I have been partying all day because it's Philip Honour's birthday. I must remember to make sure he is included on the New Year's honours list, and get Mother to send him a telegram for next year's birthday.

Sunday 4th February

What a day I've had today. William and Harry came for a visit – they've recently joined the boy scouts. All day long they have been practising tying knots on me in order to earn a badge. However, by about 3 p.m. I was tied up so much that neither the boys nor myself could get them undone. In the end we had to call the fire brigade. They seemed to find it highly amusing and asked if this was 'The Princes Trussed.'

Monday 5th February

The man came to see the corgi today as arranged. I thought it odd that he didn't bring a dog with him and assumed these things were now done by artificial insemination. I showed him into the boiler house where we keep the dog kennels and he said he would be an hour or two, so I left him to it. When I returned I found him tampering with our gas boiler and assumed he was a terrorist trying to plant a bomb, so I immediately had him arrested.

Tuesday 6th February

I had a visit from the police today concerning the terrorist. It seems he claimed to be a gas engineer who had come to service the boiler. Luckily I still had the newspaper advertisement which quite clearly said 'CORGI-registered, servicing done at reasonable rates'.

Wednesday 7th February

It turns out the man knew nothing at all about corgis and was a gas engineer. I have decided not to prosecute him under the trades description act. He can consider himself lucky I chose to have him arrested and didn't follow my first instinct which was to shoot him.

Thursday 8th February

Had a phone call from Diana today. She wanted to let me know she was going to spend a few days in the sun next week. She mysteriously added she wouldn't see me for a few days but I would see her. I said I was sure she deserved a break after all her hard work. I suppose it was my sarcastic tone that made her hang up on me.

Friday 9th February

I asked Mother today if there was any chance of me becoming king this year. "Over my dead body," was her reply. She did however suggest I stop moping about at home and see if the college had any courses to interest me. I phoned the college and someone there said there were courses to suit everyone and that a prospectus would be sent in the post.

Saturday 10th February

Excellent service by the Royal Mail – my prospectus arrived today. If I can find out which part of the royal family runs the Royal Mail I must congratulate them. However, I was very disappointed with the college courses on offer as there were no courses on offer which covered my special interests of adultery or murdering poor defenceless animals.

Sunday 11th February

Although there was nothing suitable for myself at the college, I think I will enrol Father in the course – 'English as a foreign language', and Mother on a pre-retirement course.

Monday 12th February

I was absolutely stunned this morning, with Diana out of the way I thought I was in for a peaceful few days. It turns out her few days in the sun was the newspaper and not the Bahamas. Mother has always said Diana had some front, but I don't expect it all to be displayed so openly on page 3. I'm dreading tomorrow's paper when they say more will be revealed.

Tuesday 13th February

I'm deeply hurt by Diana's allegations in today's paper that I committed adultery. I have never been unfaithful to either Camilla or Diana. I can remember how pleased Camilla was when I decided to marry Diana. She even said how nice it would be for her to have somebody to chat to in our king-sized bed whenever I was away on official duties.

Wednesday 14th February

I take back my praise of the Royal Mail, as I was expecting a sackful of Valentine cards today, but they failed to deliver any. More cutting remarks in the paper today from Diana. She said I was always too busy with Bowles to find time for her.

Thursday 15th February

This week just gets worse and worse. Today Diana has admitted to the whole world that she had an affair with a chap called James Hewitt. It's true what they say – the husband is always the last to know. Mother is furious with all these revelations. I think she might send Anne round to sort Diana out.

Friday 16th February

I still can't believe that Diana could keep Mr Hewitt a secret from me. All the time I was concerned about Arthur Fowler's affair with Mrs Hewitt in *Eastenders*, I never guessed that Diana was doing the same with Mrs Hewitt's husband. Perhaps I should have an affair with Pauline Fowler to even things up.

Saturday 17th February

The last day of Diana's newspaper stories. Today she has shattered the illusion of our fairytale wedding. She says only two things made it like a fairytale – the first, that it was Grimm, and the second that she felt like Goldilocks in that she knew who'd been sleeping in her bed.

Sunday 18th February

The Prime Minister got in touch today. Members of his party are concerned about the newspaper revelations and some have even suggested that I'm not fit to be a future king of England. It is a relief that such a scandal-free government has so much faith in me.

Monday 19th February

I really enjoyed myself today as it was Andrew's birthday. It gave me a chance to get my own back on him for the present he gave me at Christmas. I'll never forgive him for giving me that *Panorama* video, especially as he had cunningly disguised it in *The Little Princess* video case.

Tuesday 20th February

Pancake Day today – one of my favourite days of the year. We always have a get-together each year and have a pancake tossing competition. I have proved I am the greatest tosser the royal family has ever had.

Wednesday 21st February

Andrew called to thank me for his birthday present which consisted of a gift voucher for Relate and a book entitled *How to Get Rid of Unwanted Accountants*. He didn't see the funny side and has decided to give me up for Lent.

Thursday 22nd February

Mother is concerned that the situation between myself and Diana is worsening so she has invited her and the boys to tea on Saturday. I wonder if I should invite Camilla in order to make it a proper family occasion.

Friday 23rd February

It has been a very hectic day today as Mother is determined that tomorrow's tea party is going to reunite Diana and myself. I was ordered out into the back garden to shoot a couple of pheasants and a deer for the occasion although I told Mother that, judging from the photographs, Diana doesn't need to put any more meat on her.

Saturday 24th February

Not a very successful day. I think I may have upset Diana when I asked her when she had her implants done. I also asked her if she was trying to compete with the other Mrs Windsor (Barbara). She told Mother she would never get back together with me and that she would rather die first. Mother retorted that beheading could still be arranged. This would have the added benefit of helping Diana lose weight. After tea, the boys wanted to play a game so we all joined in 'happy families'.

Sunday 25th February

After the trauma of yesterday Camilla and I spent the day in bed. She tried to comfort me and in fact had a good suggestion to make in order to resolve the situation. She suggested I treat Diana the same way as I treated the last princess I loved. Thinking back I recall many years ago, the love of my life was an Austin Princess and when she was past her best, I took her to the scrapyard. It's certainly worth considering, although it seems such a shame especially as the 'bodywork' is still in excellent condition.

Monday 26th February

It's only Monday and already Father is complaining that we are likely to be eating leftover pheasant all week, the remains of Saturday's fiasco. I suggested we send it to Anne. Father says she eats like a horse and will eat anything.

Tuesday 27th February

Another wet dreary day again today, made worse as usual by Mother's comment – "Reigning again dear," when she brought my breakfast to my room.

I replied, "This reign is likely to last for ever."

She said, "Yes, I probably will."

Wednesday 28th February

What a bombshell Diana dropped on me today when she announced to the whole of the world's press that she wanted a divorce. What grounds could she possibly have? I think she may have been reading that book, *Easy Ways to Become a Millionaire*. Father thinks she has finally gone mad and that we should have her put in an institution. Mother commented that marriage was an institution into which she had been committed for life.

Thursday 29th February

I was still reeling from the shock of yesterday's announcement when I had a phone call from Diana. "Charles," she said (at least we are still on first name terms), "I've got a proposal for you." Realising what day it was I quickly hung up and left the phone off the hook. If she phoned again she would find out that I was already engaged.

Friday 1st March

Mother suggested that after all I had gone through perhaps it would be a good idea if I went away for a few days. As it is St David's Day I thought perhaps a trip to Wales might be appropriate, especially as I hadn't been there since 1969.

Saturday 2nd March

After studying the map, I discovered that Wales was an undeveloped country to the west of us. So myself and an interpreter set off on the train from Paddington, daffodils in button holes to indicate we had come as friends. I wore a sturdy pair of boots as I was unsure as to whether the train service went further than Bristol.

Sunday 3rd March

I was surprised as most of the locals speak the Queen's English almost as well as myself. They are also very concerned about a visitor's comfort. Even when dishing out my main course my host asked if I wanted a leek. But I always make sure I go before I sit down to eat.

Monday 4th March

I'm beginning to enjoy my stay here in the Welsh valleys. It is so peaceful and there are many different trees and plants to talk to. If Mother is not yet ready to retire, I may ask her if she will hand over just Wales to me, so I could become King of Wales.

Tuesday 5th March

I've had second thoughts about becoming King of Wales. The one major drawback is there already appears to be a Princess of Wales. I have heard it said that Wales has a large mining community and the locals have taken to Princess Diana because they think she's the pits. I must say I'm now inclined to agree with them.

Wednesday 6th March

I have really enjoyed my short break away, but it's always nice to return to your own little home. Camilla said she missed me but that it gave her the opportunity to spend a few days with her husband.

Thursday 7th March

I've been told that today is International Women's Day, whatever that means. In our house it seems that every day is International Women's Day. Still, that's one thing I'll change when I'm in control. John Major had the right idea when he got rid of Margaret Thatcher.

Friday 8th March

We've been discussing a family holiday today. We don't often get the chance to get away and it is difficult to decide where to go. Father as always wants to go to Corfu. I fancy staying in England as there is less chance of bumping into Diana in this country. Mother thinks we should go to Cornwall, because I own it and it would be cheap.

Saturday 9th March

Busy day again – tomorrow is Edward's birthday. As he's the baby of the family, Mother always lays on a party for him. She has been busy making jellies all day. Mother is really proud of him because he has managed to get a job and always sends a few bob home when times are hard.

Sunday 10th March

As usual on Edward's birthday, the party is fancy dress. Being an actor he always enjoys dressing up. The only rule about the costume was they had to be as far removed from reality as possible. That was why Fergie came as a beautiful princess, Camilla as the Queen, whilst Mother dressed up as the Australian Prime Minister. Father wore a smart suit – his chance to wear the trousers in our household, and I dressed as an anti-bloodsport campaigner.

Monday 11th March

Edward couldn't stay for long as he had to return to the theatre where he is rehearsing for a starring role in a musical. He was sorry to have to take off the cowboy outfit I had bought him for his birthday and put on his normal clothes of platform shoes and sequinned jacket. These theatrical types are all the same aren't they, darling?

Tuesday 12th March

There seems to be a lot of talk about abolishing the monarchy again recently. It would be just my luck for this to happen halfway through my coronation. There is talk that many people favour the election of a president rather than having a king or queen. Perhaps I'd better write an election campaign speech just in case.

Wednesday 13th March

In preparation for a presidential election campaign, I phoned ex-President Reagan to find out how he and Nancy prepared for their successful election, but unfortunately he couldn't remember. In fact he didn't even remember who Nancy was. I think perhaps I should appoint a campaign manager – someone who could build up my popularity with the public.

Thursday 14th March

My understanding of the president's role in Britain is that it should not be based on political beliefs. Perhaps Paddy Ashdown would make an ideal adviser. I think it always helps to win popular support if you appear in public with a pretty girl on your arm. I must remember to ask Camilla if she knows of anybody who may be suitable for me.

Friday 15th March

Anne visited today. We had a lucky escape because we heard the rattle of her collection tin as she approached the front door, so we all hid until she went away. Last time she came we couldn't get rid of her until we'd filled up two tins. Still, we managed to get rid of quite a few of Father's drachmas.

Saturday 16th March

Saturday nights don't seem quite the same as they used to. I used to always enjoy playing cards with the rest of the family but the games don't seem the same nowadays because Mother insists the queen of hearts is removed from the pack.

Sunday 17th March

Mother's Day today so we decided to take Mother out for a meal. She didn't seem to appreciate my choice of venue though (the King Charles Inn). After the meal we returned to watch a video called *Some Mothers Do Ave 'Em* – an amusing story of a family called Spencer who get into all sorts of difficulties. Rather true to life, I thought.

Monday 18th March

An article in one of the national newspapers upset Mother today. It seems they are mounting an 'Abolish the Monarchy' campaign and to gauge the people's feelings they are running a telephone poll on one of those 0898 numbers, where the price of a call at cheap rate is enough to bankrupt the nation.

Tuesday 19th March

Mother is jubilant. By an overwhelming majority the newspaper had to concede defeat. The telephone poll was more than eighty per cent in favour of the monarchy remaining. I hope she will still be as pleased when she gets the next telephone bill, as it took me all day yesterday on the phone to get that result.

Wednesday 20th March

I noticed that Father seemed rather depressed and he admitted he had hoped that Mother would lose the poll and that the monarchy would be abolished so we could all lead ordinary lives. It turns out his phone calls were the other twenty per cent of the poll.

Thursday 21st March

Camilla has been a bit of a nuisance lately. She seems to feel she should be given a title like Diana was. She has got it into her head that Lady Camilla sounds right. I upset her by saying I thought the title of 'lady' was stretching the imagination a bit far. Mistress Camilla would more adequately describe her position.

Friday 22nd March

It seems that with Mother's 'victory' in the opinion polls, I am able to put off my preparations for the presidency for a while. A pity in some ways because in view of Diana's recent revelations, I was considering her for the position of vice-president, seeing as vice appears to be something she is proficient at.

Saturday 23rd March

William and Harry are spending the weekend with me. I thought they were now old enough to learn about some of the responsibilities the royal family has to bear. I took them out into the countryside where I explained there was a danger of a population explosion of partridges and pheasants. I therefore showed them how to keep the numbers down.

Sunday 24th March

Another beautiful day so I decided to put it to good use and let the boys practise some more game shooting. Harry said he had heard that Auntie Sarah was fair game and a good sport – should he therefore shoot her? It was a tempting idea.

Monday 25th March

Today is the start of several days' celebration in our household. Being a very patriotic family, we always celebrate Greek Independence Day. Father always organises a street party although surprisingly it never seems to catch on in the rest of the country. I am considering declaring it a national holiday.

Tuesday 26th March

Everybody seems to be getting into the mood of the event this year but I'm glad Diana wasn't invited. Last year, we were all supposed to wear authentic costumes of Greece but she was the only one who came dressed as Olivia Newton-John. It is always a thrill to see the pride on Father's face as he raises the Greek flag on the palace roof.

Wednesday 27th March

The last day of the festival today which was marred as usual when Father went off in a huff after going through our photo albums. It has always upset him that I chose to play polo for England and not Greece. Mother tried to pacify him by promising that if I ever entered the Eurovision Song Contest I would represent Greece. Having heard my singing this upset him even more.

Thursday 28th March

I heard a new record today by the Beatles which I find amazing considering they split up in 1970 and John Lennon was murdered in 1980. One wonders if this could happen in other walks of life. Perhaps twenty years after Diana and I split up she could still be producing further heirs to the throne.

Friday 29th March

Mother has been complaining of having a bad headache for the last few days. I suggested to her that the crown may be getting too heavy for her and offered what I thought was a reasonable solution, but she declined and took a couple of aspirins.

Saturday 30th March

So Diana has had another affair, this time with Will Carling – she's certainly playing the field. Again I think I should have spotted the signs as it seemed every time I answered the door he was there with the excuse he'd kicked his ball into our back garden.

Sunday 31st March

The start of British Summer Time. It always takes me about three hours to go around the palace altering all the clocks. There is at least one in every room, so I usually lose four hours instead of one. Except last year, when I put the clocks back instead of forward wasting virtually the whole day. I wish I could put the clocks back about fifteen years instead of one hour forward – back to when I was young, single and still unemployed.

Monday 1st April

April Fool's Day. What a brilliant joke the local council played on us today. They sent us council tax demands for every one of our homes. I suggested to Mother that we return them marked 'not known at this address'.

Tuesday 2nd April

After reading the council tax small print, it seems we don't have to pay after all. Properties that are unoccupied for more than six months of the year are exempt. As we are away on holiday for at least eight months a year, we can get away with it.

Wednesday 3rd April

My good friend Will Carling is in Mother's good books. In fact he may even be in line for a knighthood because by admitting his affair with Diana he has probably saved me at least five million pounds in divorce settlement. If I can get the rest of the England team to also claim they had affairs with Diana she could even end up owing me.

Thursday 4th April

Maundy Thursday – a day traditionally hated by monarchy because of having to give the Maundy money of £1 to the poor for every year of the reign. Another reason for Mother to abdicate because if I took over I wouldn't have to give anything away this year.

Friday 5th April

Good Friday. I enjoy hot cross buns which always remind me of the day Jesus was crucified. If this tradition were to be extended to commemorate the number of times the royal family had been crucified by the press, I'd be eating hot cross buns virtually every day.

Saturday 6th April

Saturday night is always a time I look forward to as it provides yet another chance to pay Diana off. But today, once again I was to be disappointed. If only I'd used my instinct and picked Will Carling's shirt number, I would have won a tenner – more than enough to have paid Diana off considering recent events.

Sunday 7th April

Easter Sunday and I'm afraid I had to disappoint the boys. I refuse to buy them Easter eggs on principle because they are all shaped like rugby balls. Still I think I made it up to them by giving them each a bag of royal mints – polos of course.

Monday 8th April

Easter Monday means it's another day off, therefore it's no different to any other day. We did decide to have a picnic in the back garden as it was so nice today. But halfway there the Land Rover ran out of petrol. I don't suppose ordinary people get that problem. We still managed to have our picnic and the food was delicious. I got in a temper with Father because he was in charge of the drinks and had only brought lager (Carling Black Label).

Tuesday 9th April

Another crisis appears to be looming. Several MPs have been complaining recently that the royal family costs far too much to keep. Mother has asked us if we can think of ways in which money can be saved. I can see that before long she will be cutting our pocket money.

Wednesday 10th April

It seems that certain members of the family have been taking advantage of some of the perks we get. We are all allowed to send out mail for business purposes free of charge but Sarah has been writing letters to all of her friends without paying postage. Mother has now put a stop to this and I estimate this could save the taxpayer 50p a year.

Thursday 11th April

The royal yacht *Britannia* is also going to be axed as a further cost-cutting exercise. Mother is due to sail to France shortly and in the past it has been traditional for her to host a banquet on the *Britannia* in honour of other heads of state. Her new itinerary has now been amended to include the grandeur of a buffet on board the cross channel ferry.

Friday 12th April

Mother organised a family meeting today to discuss financial matters. It has been rumoured that cash paid to the family from the civil list may soon be drastically cut. Mother has sent us away to think of ways that money could be saved or additional money raised.

Saturday 13th April

It is said that the royal family brings many foreign tourists to London each year, but I don't see any of the cash benefits personally. I think I'll suggest to Mother that we rent out some of our spare rooms or even spare homes to these people in order to generate extra cash. I might even persuade Mother to act as landlady and provide bed and breakfast.

Sunday 14th April

I've been thinking more about this bed and breakfast idea and think it could be a winner. We could even promote it further by selling souvenirs. We could sell T shirts emblazoned with the slogan 'I've slept in Princess Diana's bed' – although I don't suppose there would be much of a novelty in that.

Monday 15th April

I'm coming up with more fund-raising ideas every day – I'm sure Mother will be pleased. Today I thought perhaps Andrew could give helicopter flying lessons around the palace grounds. His souvenir T shirts could say 'I've handled Andrew's chopper'.

Tuesday 16th April

If my bed and breakfast idea takes off, Mother may not be able to cope on her own. She could even employ Diana and Sarah to help out. We could even advertise that 'Diana and Sarah cater for your every need.' Alternatively we could provide self-catering accommodation where by the end of your stay you could be half-bored by the Queen.

Wednesday 17th April

I've been wondering how Anne could raise money and as she is involved in charity work it would be easy for her to get her hands on some collecting tins. She could start a door-to-door collection as they say that charity always begins at home. She could name the charity 'Now Assist Failing Funds of Royal Family' – NAFFORF for short.

Thursday 18th April

I am also considering trying to organise appropriate sponsorship deals for individual members of the family. For instance, to help with Diana's numerous trips abroad. Perhaps Virgin Airways would sponsor her trips. On second thoughts they do have an image to protect.

Friday 19th April

Good news. I have already managed to find Father a sponsor. I thought he was going to be difficult but a famous violin manufacturer is willing to support him as they are always keen to help anybody who has been playing second fiddle for as long as Father has.

Saturday 20th April

More sponsorship deals agreed today – our local butcher has agreed to sponsor Edward. He has taken into account Edward's acting ability and thinks Edward would be ideal for promoting his ham rolls.

Sunday 21st April

It seems very unfair. It's Mother's birthday today but I don't see why she should get two each year especially as the rest of the family are finding it hard to make ends meet. I'm not quite sure how old she is – either one hundred and forty or three score years and ten. Either way I'm sure it must be my turn now.

I hear that Mother is not the only one celebrating her seventieth today; Diana is also (first was me, second was James Hewitt, third Will Carling, etc., etc., etc.).

Monday 22nd April

I forgot to mention yesterday what I got Mother for her birthday. I thought I'd get her something useful this year, so after reading newspaper reports that the crown had been somewhat tarnished lately, I decided to buy her a tin of Brasso.

Tuesday 23rd April

Although the family has no real reason to celebrate I understand the rest of the country today celebrates St George's day. I have heard he is the patron saint of England and that he became famous after slaying a dragon. Could that be the reason why Margaret Thatcher hasn't called around here recently?

Wednesday 24th April

Back to cost-cutting today. Mother has decided that more cuts need to be made so she has announced that two carriages from the royal train are to be sold off. I intend to make sure that Diana is still on board at the time of sale. It seems the train and our marriage have both run out of steam.

Thursday 25th April

It is proving extremely hard to find a suitable sponsor for Mother but at last I think I have done it. At first I thought I had been successful in attracting the Meteorological Office but after giving it some thought, they decided they would be even more unpopular if associated with a prolonged period of reign.

Friday 26th April

I may have failed in the end to get Mother a sponsor but she did manage to get one herself. When I asked her who it was she replied, "Wilkinson Sword." I couldn't see why they would be suitable until Mother explained they were well known for getting rid of unwanted heirs.

Saturday 27th April

It's amazing the interest that has arisen out of my sponsorship idea. Today the British Egg Marketing Board contacted me and they are willing to pay handsomely if we approve their idea. They want to print Diana's picture on to all of their eggs along with their slogan, 'Freshly laid today'.

Sunday 28th April

After all my work over the past couple of weeks I decided to have a well-earned day of rest. Mother brought me breakfast in bed as usual but she couldn't understand why I burst out into uncontrollable laughter at the sight of my hard-boiled egg.

Monday 29th April

I think I'll leave the sponsorship idea for a while as Mother is keen for me to try to think up other ways of raising much-needed revenue. I've considered ways in which other companies or charities raise money and I am wondering whether I could organise something along the lines of Comic Relief's Red Nose Day – perhaps White Ears Day or something similar.

Tuesday 30th April

I've had second thoughts about White Ears Day. Father thought it was a great idea as it would be funny to see the whole country wearing huge floppy white Prince Charles ears. He even suggested running a fete in the garden and that I could run a white elephant stall. It wouldn't even cost me anything as I wouldn't need to go out and buy the ears.

Wednesday 1st May

Oh dear! I've been out-voted. The rest of the family think White Ears Day is a great idea and will probably bring in millions. I'm concerned that it could make the royal family, especially me, a laughing-stock. But then again I don't suppose there is anything new in that.

Thursday 2nd May

Things are really moving now. It has been decided that to make White Ears Day more authentic my ears should be used as a model, so I have had a most uncomfortable day with both ears encased in plaster of paris. Having the plaster on did have one consolation though... it meant I couldn't hear everybody laughing at me.

Friday 3rd May

I've had the first pair of White Ears sent to me today for approval. Owing to their size, I think it quite reasonable for the price to be set at about £10 a pair. As they are my size, I think I will ask for a flesh-coloured pair to be made for me so I could wear them in the summer to stop my real ones getting sunburnt.

Saturday 4th May

Anne visited me today so I showed the ears to her – she was very impressed. She has always been a very practical person and she thought that unlike the red noses, these need not be thrown away after use. She suggested they could be used as jelly moulds to enable the public to produce their own royal jelly. I think I'll increase the price to £20 a pair.

Sunday 5th May

William and Harry came to see me today which was nice as I hadn't seen them recently. I put the ears on because I wanted their opinion of them. Children can be so hurtful... I wore those ears all day and they didn't even notice.

Monday 6th May

Spring Bank Holiday today which I can appreciate for the first time. Usually every day seems the same but after having worked for the last couple of weeks I really enjoyed having a restful day off. When I'm king, I think that every Monday will be an official holiday.

Tuesday 7th May

Back to work today to try to work out more fund-raising ideas for the big day. I think it is probably best to stick to tried and tested methods. Obviously, making a record can bring in plenty of money, especially if each member of the family will sing a track.

Wednesday 8th May

I have been giving serious thought to the songs which are to appear on our record. I have already decided to sing *Reigning In My Heart*. Diana will no doubt want to do *Who Wants To Be A Millionaire?* I must make sure she doesn't get any royalties. Sarah and Andrew could sing a duet as it's a long time since they did anything together. No, on second thoughts, Sarah does a rather good version of *Big Spender*.

Thursday 9th May

More album track planning today – and it's surprising how long it takes. It doesn't help when Mother refuses to let Father sing *I'm the Leader of the Gang*. I have managed to enlist Aunt Margaret though – she promised me a fine rendition of *Smoke Gets in Your Eyes*.

Friday 10th May

I've got Mother sorted out now. She will perform *I Will Survive* – no doubt the extended mix – while she has instructed Father to sing *Every Little Thing She Does is Magic*. Edward will do *Gonna Make You a Star*, and Andrew a fine rendition of *Soldier Blue* – assisted by Sarah.

Saturday 11th May

Cup Final day. Another of those events I am expected to attend but know nothing about. This year is different as we need the money and I have managed to sell both mine and Mother's tickets. I sold Mother's very easily as it gave Margaret Thatcher the chance of playing the queen she has always wanted to be. What I didn't mention was that I sold the other ticket to Edward Heath. It should make for an interesting afternoon and I might even be tempted to watch on television.

Sunday 12th May

The boys came today, eager to see if there was anything they could do to help raise money. It made me really proud to feel that when the chips were down, they would be willing to help. I later found out that their mother had put them up to it because she was worried about their inheritance.

Monday 13th May

I've just realised I've been working for a whole month now, which must be some sort of a record – I must be due some holiday soon. I broached the subject with Mother but she said she will not allow too many of the family to be away on holiday at the same time. However, I am allowed to go once Sarah and Diana return from theirs. I estimate I will have to wait for about six months.

Tuesday 14th May

I'm becoming a bit concerned about all this talk of a single European currency. If there's a referendum I will certainly vote against it. Imagine opening your wallet and seeing a picture of someone else's parents on your banknotes.

Wednesday 15th May

Where would it all end? It might start with banknotes but who says it wouldn't spread. We could end up with the European postage stamp. It makes me feel quite ill at the thought of having to lick the back of a German or Frenchman's head. There would be no point in becoming king if I couldn't have my picture on everything.

Thursday 16th May

If Mother's picture was to be removed from things, would the public remember who she was – would her speech at Christmas cease to exist or would it become a European speech spoken in a common language by a European leader? It just doesn't bear thinking about that we might even have to pretend we actually like the Germans.

Friday 17th May

Had to do something to take my mind off all these European fears I have, so I went outside to do some gardening. Mother had mentioned that we were getting rather low on potatoes so I dug a few pounds for her – King Edwards of course. Perish the thought that they could be renamed King Juan Carlos or something equally awful.

Saturday 18th May

After having enjoyed some time in the garden yesterday, I decided to spend some more time there today. Father also had the same idea but I was absolutely horrified to see that he had planted Brussels sprouts, French beans and Spanish onions in our English country garden.

Sunday 19th May

As it is Sunday today, I thought I would take it easy – have a leisurely breakfast with the rest of the family; only to find them all eating croissants. I pointed out the error of their ways and we all had a traditional English fry-up. It seems we are all becoming Europeans without realising it. I'm determined to remain British through and through. Couldn't be bothered to cook myself lunch today so I went out for a pizza.

Monday 20th May

Most of the fund-raising ideas for White Ears Day are now well in progress so I will have to find something else to do to fill up my time. I think I shall start a 'Keep Everything British Campaign'. Come to think of it, by keeping things British I could also be helping to save money. I'm going to start banning all foreign heads of state from coming to the palace and scrounging our hospitality.

Tuesday 21st May

Mother thinks I'm taking this British theme too far as I'm now refusing to eat New Zealand lamb or turkey. I don't think you can eat anything better than British beef. Mother commented that Diana restricted herself to British beef whilst on one of her diets and she is convinced that she's now suffering from Mad Cow Disease.

Wednesday 22nd May

I've just had a brilliant idea! I think this country should become self-sufficient. I've already suggested we close all airports and fill in the Channel Tunnel. This would have other benefits if done immediately, bearing in mind that both Diana and Sarah are out of the country at the moment.

Thursday 23rd May

I'm really enjoying concentrating on being British and I've been getting support from Mother over the past few days. She has insisted that only British food is served here. Unfortunately this situation does not please everybody as Father has been suffering Greek food withdrawal symptoms and I have heard him cursing in his native tongue.

Friday 24th May

I had a visit from the Greek Ambassador today. It seems now that Father has been ordered to eat only British food, the three local Greek takeaways have been forced to close owing to lack of trade. Not only has this forced the shopkeepers to sell up and return to Greece but it has also cost Father his secret job as part-time waiter.

Saturday 25th May

I received a 'Glad You're Not Here' card from Diana today. It seems she managed to buy a ticket for the England rugby tour. From what I can gather, she is playing her usual position – hooker! She says it is proving to be a very cheap holiday especially as she borrowed my credit card without my knowledge or consent.

Sunday 26th May

I've reported my credit card as stolen and I can't wait, because the police say that next time somebody tries to use it they will be arrested. I did forget to mention that I knew who had taken it. I wonder if she will still be able to claim a divorce settlement whilst detained at Her Majesty's pleasure?

Monday 27th May

Well that didn't take long. I had a call from the police to say a lady had been arrested for trying to use my card. I opposed bail which means she will remain in custody until she appears in court on Friday. It's moments like that which make it all worthwhile.

Tuesday 28th May

Mother said that I had seemed so much happier for the past couple of days. I told her about Diana's arrest and she thinks that when she's been convicted, I should apply for custody of the boys as it would not be in the best interests of the country for my son, the future king of England, and his brother to live with a criminal.

Wednesday 29th May

With all the excitement of the past few days I completely forgot that Monday was another bank holiday. Still one consolation, Diana will have missed it as well and it must be the first time that she's missed out on a holiday, although she is still getting full board at the moment.

Thursday 30th May

Something has gone terribly wrong. Diana called round today to remind me we had a parents' evening to attend at the boys' school on Monday. I asked her what she was doing out already. She just looked at me as if I was mad, and then left.

Friday 31st May

Today was supposed to be the day I had been looking forward to all week – the day Diana was convicted of credit card fraud. However, I was stunned when I turned on the early evening news to hear the headline – 'Camilla convicted of fraud!' It seems that Diana had called round last Sunday to return my card but I was out. She left it with Camilla who then used the bally thing on Monday when she went to collect and pay for some dry-cleaning for me.

Saturday 1st June

The situation has now become extremely awkward for me. After my divorce comes through I had intended to marry Camilla but now I don't know if I should be seen fraternising with a known criminal. I shall definitely have to give the matter some more serious thought.

Sunday 2nd June

Camilla is not a happy woman. She said she could have coped with the embarrassment of being arrested in a case of mistaken identity, but it really upset her when I insisted on pressing charges and then opposing bail. She had always been delighted to be a guest of the Queen, but had never anticipated being forcibly detained on Her Majesty's premises.

Monday 3rd June

The boys seem to be doing very well at school at the moment. Their teacher feels they may be able to have a career in the sporting line. Their sports master asked me if I had been giving them extra coaching at home. I was proud to reply that I encouraged them to play polo at every opportunity. He said he was not referring to polo but to their amazing progress at rugby.

Tuesday 4th June

Before we left the school yesterday, we were handed the boys' reports. The headmaster commented that both boys were showing fine leadership qualities and had been made captains of their respective forms. They were also excelling at sports, especially rugby. It is hard to see who they take after.

Wednesday 5th June

The more I think about the school reports the more it worries me. Neither of the lads seem to take after me at all. They are doing well at things like sport but when it comes to languages, especially Greek, it doesn't seem to come naturally to them at all.

Thursday 6th June

Another thought has struck me today, thinking back to when our eldest was born. I could never work out why Diana was against naming him Charles. She was most insistent he should be called William although she would never say why.

Friday 7th June

I've always known that Diana loved William far more than she ever loved me. She used to refer to him as her little darling. At least I thought it was darling she's said, or might it have been something other than Will darling that I'd heard.

Saturday 8th June

If has been more than a week since Camilla's trial, but she still hasn't forgiven me. I think I will have to do something really special for her to get back into her good books. I'll speak to Mother about it as she owns the prisons and I'm sure she could arrange for Camilla to have her own private cell.

Sunday 9th June

Good news! Mother has managed to arrange for Camilla to be released and instead of having to stay in prison, she will now only have to pay a fine. I'm sure she will be delighted and it will also save me from baking a cake and putting a file in it.

Monday 10th June

Talk about ungrateful. Camilla came to see me today and I thought I would get some thanks for making sure she only had to serve a short sentence. Instead she gave me a short sentence of her own. It consisted of just two little words.

Tuesday 11th June

I don't know – I just don't seem to be able to do anything right at present as far as Camilla is concerned. Today I called to see her and as a peace offering I said I would pay her fine for her. She seemed to accept the offer at first and for a while we were back on friendly terms. But this all changed when I gave her my credit card to pay the fine with.

Wednesday 12th June

We seem to be having difficulty in obtaining new staff for palace security at the moment. Mother is blaming me because she says that nobody wants to work for a family which seems to always get bad publicity.

Thursday 13th June

I've just seen the recruitment advertisement that Mother is using. It's no wonder she can't get staff; her advert reads as follows. 'Wanted – Beefeaters who are prepared to stand outside the palace for hours on end in their bearskins'. Surely she must know nobody eats beef these days.

Friday 14th June

Camilla and I are on speaking terms again thank goodness, although she was still angry with me at first until I told her I would give her anything to be friends again. She said she didn't want more than she deserved or felt she was entitled to. I was amazed when I found out all she wanted was twelve and a half pence. If only Diana would take a leaf out of her book.

Saturday 15th June

Once again I've got it wrong. I misunderstood what Camilla had asked for and now I feel a proper Charlie. I thought she was being an old fashioned girl when she said she just wanted half a crown (which I converted to new money). What she wanted was half of my crown – she wants to be queen.

Sunday 16th June

I thought I'd been forgotten by the boys today. I was sure that it being Father's Day, they would spend most of the day with me, but they didn't turn up until six o'clock this evening. They said that with all of the different dads they had had over the last few years, they didn't know who to visit first.

Monday 17th June

I've talked over the problem of Camilla becoming queen with Mother but unfortunately she is against it. She says if I want to be king I must remain single. The only reason she paid for Diana and myself to get married was so that we could have children to carry on the family name.

Tuesday 18th June

Camilla was extremely angry when I broke the news to her that Mother would not allow her to marry me and become queen, and she's not a pretty sight when she's angry – come to think of it she's not a pretty sight when she's happy either. Now I don't know if I should marry Camilla and upset Mother or stay single and upset Camilla.

Wednesday 19th June

Today I've made a decision. I will marry Camilla as she did manage to persuade me it would be in my best interests. In fact she did twist my arm – so much I thought it was going to break.

Thursday 20th June

We've decided not to tell Mother about our wedding plans yet especially as I'm not even divorced. I've also decided not to tell Camilla I don't intend to get married until after my coronation. But I'm not too keen about Camilla retaining her surname after the wedding. She wants us to be known as Charles and Camilla Parker-Bowles-Windsor. It's a name with more barrels than my favourite hunting gun.

Friday 21st June

I think it's my eldest son's birthday today; when I say I think it is, I mean I know it's William's birthday but I'm not sure he's my eldest son. I spoke to him on the phone today and he said he would be coming to see me tomorrow and I would be able to give him his present then.

Saturday 22nd June

William visited as promised and so I gave him his present. I wanted him to have something very special so I let him have my favourite hunting gun which has been in the family for many generations. He seemed delighted with it and spent a couple of hours in the garden trying it out.

Sunday 23rd June

Diana phoned and let me have it with all guns blazing so to speak. She was not at all happy with my choice of present for William. She thinks he should be brought up looking after animals and protecting them. I think what really upset her was William shooting the rabbit she had bought him for a pet for his birthday. I think William is definitely my son after all.

Monday 24th June

I decided it was time to have a holiday. I thought I might spend a few days away with Camilla so I asked her where she would like to go and she said Queensland. I don't know what she was hinting at, but I said we must be patriotic and stay in Britain. In the end I opted to go to Cornwall, mainly because I thought I might get a staff discount.

Tuesday 25th June

We arrived at our hotel today and booked in as Mr and Mrs Smith so the press would not get wind of our visit. Camilla loves our room and said it would make the ideal place for a honeymoon – she never gives up does she? I think the landlady suspects we are not who we say we are. Signing in as Charles must have given the game away I'm sure.

Wednesday 26th June

Spent the day looking at local architecture which was Camilla's idea. Somehow we ended up in a very quaint church which was all prepared for a wedding. Even the priest seemed to expect us. I think Camilla may have set this up because she said it seemed pointless to waste the opportunity. I did have to point out to her the minor point that I was still married. She countered with, "Well, I read that King Henry had six wives." What she didn't realise was that they were not all at the same time.

Thursday 27th June

Went to the beach today and built my own castle just so that I could play at being king of it. We also went to the local art gallery where they featured landscapes of all parts of the British Isles. Camilla bought one of the Gower coast and another of Snowdonia because they reminded her of me – they were both prints of Wales.

Friday 28th June

We had a tour of the coastline today on the open-top bus. It was quite a windy day and Camilla's hair looked an absolute mess after the trip. Funny thing is though it didn't seem to affect my hairstyle at all.

Saturday 29th June

We've decided we will return home tomorrow as I'm sure the landlady knows who we are. She has started using the best silver and curtsying whenever she serves us meals. I think the royal crest on my suitcase may have given us away.

Sunday 30th June

Well, Mr and Mrs Smith have booked out of the hotel and have now arrived back home safely. Our landlady has agreed to keep our stay a secret provided I send her 10,000 pictures of Mother as featured on the £50 note. I told her the royals no longer have that sort of money and threatened to send Anne there for her holidays if she says anything.

Monday 1st July

Halfway through another year and I still hold the same title I was given on the 1st July 1969 when I was made The Prince of Wales. Isn't it funny how the initials are the same as for 'Prisoner of War'? I don't think it is a coincidence as I've felt trapped ever since.

Tuesday 2nd July

I was right – I thought that would annoy her. Not only was the 1st July an important date for me but it was also an important day for Mr and Mrs Spencer as their daughter Diana was born on that day in 1961. Diana rang me today annoyed that I had forgotten to send her a birthday card, but I assured her I hadn't forgotten, I just didn't bother.

Wednesday 3rd July

Mother is still very concerned about the royal finances so she has again decided to open Buckingham Palace to the public next month. In order to give it maximum publicity we have decided the palace opening will coincide with White Ears Day on Saturday 10th August.

Thursday 4th July

American Independence Day. I think I should have a Charles Independence Day – a day that I could forget about Mother and do exactly as I please or perhaps the whole family could become independent and not have to rely on state handouts or charities.

Friday 5th July

I have read rumours in the press that Diana has got yet another boyfriend although he has not been named. It has been suggested he is a famous pop singer. I'll bet it's Prince – or could it be a member of the group Queen. She'll go out with anyone who has even a tenuous royal connection. In fact, before we met she dated all of the corgis.

Saturday 6th July

This time I was wrong. Diana has not been seeing Prince. The pop singer rumoured to be her latest flame is Chris Rea. I'm sure she'll take him down the road to hell. Mind you, if they do stay together it could save me some money in the divorce settlement.

Sunday 7th July

I'd love Diana's latest romance to last. Can you imagine what would happen if they got married? I know she would never get a dinner invitation from Mother or else the invitation card might read – 'Her Majesty the Queen requests the pleasure of Di Rea for dinner'. It would probably resemble one of Father's Greek takeaways.

Monday 8th July

The boys phoned me today to ask if I would go with them to their school sports day tomorrow which was to be run on the same lines as the Olympic Games. Considering my Greek ancestry I could hardly refuse could I? Anyway if I didn't go, their mother would make sure I was for the high jump.

Tuesday 9th July

I met up with the boys and Diana at the school. It was the first time we had all been together as a family for quite some time. Harry took part in the Snickers race (it used to be called the Marathon but it didn't last long). Whilst William didn't take part in any races, he was in charge of the starter's pistol – he does take after me it seems. All went well until we had to take part in the parents sack race. I won but Diana came last. She never was any good at keeping her legs together. She wouldn't speak to me after that.

Wednesday 10th July

Father's birthday today. He is always a very difficult person to buy a present for. This year I decided I would get him a kilt. He was delighted with it and so was Mother. She got so annoyed when I bought him a pair of trousers last year because she says that she's the one who wears the trousers in this house.

Thursday 11th July

The children come home from school at the end of next week for the summer holidays. Two whole months we are expected to look after them. I don't know how ordinary parents cope as I understand that most children come home every day after lessons and don't go back until the following day.

Friday 12th July

These school holidays are really worrying me. I can find something to amuse the boys for the odd afternoon but not for weeks on end. I think I'll have to come to an agreement with Diana that we could look after them for half the time each. She could have them in the daytime and I'd have them at night when they are asleep.

Saturday 13th July

Diana and the boys came to see me today to discuss the holiday arrangements. The boys want to go on a camping holiday because this is what their friends do and they don't want to appear different. It seems I have been chosen to take them as Diana is not used to roughing it (apart from her Will Carling experience of course).

Sunday 14th July

I've decided I'll take the boys on our camping holiday from next Saturday so I can get it over with as soon as possible. I think we'll go to the Balmoral Estate so we can do a spot of fishing. If I've got to rough it, I'll rough it on Mother's best salmon.

Monday 15th July

St Swithin's Day and thank goodness it didn't rain today. That means it might remain dry for our Balmoral expedition. I can't think of anything worse than a week's camping in the rain with the boys except of course being trapped in a tent for a week with Diana. We'd have to amuse ourselves playing cards, she's very good at snap. Then again, she's had plenty of practice.

Tuesday 16th July

Camilla said she wants to come on the holiday as well. She thinks it would be a good chance to get to know the boys before she becomes their step mother. I think it might be a good idea as well because we need a strapping person to carry the kit.

Wednesday 17th July

I'm in Mother's bad books since I told her Camilla was coming on holiday with the boys and I. She doesn't think the boys should see their father carrying on, as she puts it, whilst still married to Diana. I pointed out that they had been witnessing their mother carrying on for I don't know how many years.

Thursday 18th July

Mother thinks I've compromised with my promise that Camilla and I will have separate tents whilst away, when in fact I'm quite relieved as I've not yet fully recovered from our Cornwall trip. It was a shock to the system seeing her first thing in the morning before she woke up. It made me think that although we were staying in a hotel, I still had a sleeping bag.

Friday 19th July

I was dreading the forthcoming holiday. I always thought a holiday was a time to be pampered and to be waited on hand and foot. Rather like staying at home really, and not being stranded out in the wilds fending for yourself.

Saturday 20th July

The boys arrived early, excited at the prospect of spending a week with me and who can blame them for that. We all set off for the railway station ready to board the royal train for the journey only to find that Mother had hired it out to a local football club to transport the team to an away match. It had been renamed 'The Orient Express'. Still I suppose it will bring in much-needed income. In the end all was not lost as Andrew offered to take us in his helicopter. The only drawback is that Sarah came too.

Sunday 21st July

Andrew and Sarah decided to stay on at Balmoral with us for a few days as the weather was so good. This did create a problem as we only had two tents. The women decided to share one, leaving us four lads in the other. It was a tight squeeze but somehow the girls managed it.

Monday 22nd July

We had quite a pleasant day fishing today and we were pleased with what we had caught – all except Andrew who exclaimed that all he'd caught was an old trout. I pointed out that he had brought Sarah with him and could not include her in today's catch.

Tuesday 23rd July

It's Andrew and Sarah's wedding anniversary today. They have done well to stay together although at times over the years I have sensed the atmosphere between them has been too tense. They didn't seem very happy today and when I asked Andrew what was wrong he replied, "Too tense."

I said, "You ought not to be – you should be relaxed, you're on holiday."

He said, "No, no; two tents is the problem – me in one and Sarah in another."

Wednesday 24th July

We decided to spend some time away from the camp today. Andrew offered to show us some of the local sights from his helicopter – very impressive. Sarah said it was Andrew's chopper that first attracted her to him and it has inspired her to write several books, though they did not sell very well. Her later books about Budgie the helicopter were successful though.

Thursday 25th July

William and Harry seem to be enjoying themselves and more importantly they are conducting themselves as one would expect. They get great pleasure out of shooting rabbits and other small animals and watching them slowly bleed to death. It warms my heart that the young royals will carry on our proud traditions.

Friday 26th July

Our last night away so we had a good old singsong around the camp fire. Andrew supplied the drink having bought us a six-pack of lager each. I had to refuse mine because I had already had a bellyful of Carling over the last few months.

Saturday 27th July

We returned home today after a really enjoyable week away. Mother and Father were pleased to see us, especially Father. Life had been hell for him whilst we were away because he was the only one left at home for Mother to order about. He made us promise to take him if ever we went away again.

Sunday 28th July

Diana called around today to collect the boys as it was now her turn to look after them for a while. Harry thanked me for a nice time, kissed me goodbye and then asked Diana which Daddy they were going to stay with next.

Monday 29th July

I'm not divorced yet so I suppose that today must be my wedding anniversary. Things started off badly and I should have realised it wouldn't last when Diana got my name wrong during the ceremony. Diana was never the devoted wife – she promised to obey me but then refused to let Camilla come on our honeymoon.

Tuesday 30th July

Mother is getting anxious now as White Ears Day and the palace being opened to the public is less than two weeks away. She's trying to book Father into a residential care home as she doesn't like him to be seen by the public, because anybody who upsets him is likely to hear some language from him which definitely isn't Greek.

Wednesday 31st July

Mother has ordered all the family to clean their private quarters before the public invasion. I told her I have a bath regularly, every six months, even if I don't really need one. She insisted I vacuum my room every day from now on until opening and beyond. I think I'll go into a residential home as well. Perhaps the YWCA will take me in.

Thursday 1st August

Anne came for a visit today but was most unhappy when she left. She had worn her new wellington boots but Mother made her take them off and leave them outside the gates so she didn't dirty the carpets. When it was time for her to go she found the boots had been stolen. It wasn't the fact the boots were stolen that upset her, it was Mother complaining her feet had made dirtier marks on the carpet than the boots would have done.

Friday 2nd August

Today Mother has had turnstiles fitted in the palace's main entrance ready for the paying public. The only problem with that is it's costing me £10 a time whenever I want to go in or out of my own front door. She wouldn't even give me a staff discount.

Saturday 3rd August

Father hasn't gone into the home yet and he is creating havoc here at home. Mother had been on her hands and knees all morning scrubbing the dirty marks off the carpet when Father came down the hallway in his carriage pulled by two horses, who paused to do their business on the newly cleaned carpet.

Sunday 4th August

Yesterday's incident has not yet been forgotten. Mother and Father are not speaking to each other. Father told me he was just practising his carriage racing in the hope he could qualify for the Greek Olympic team. As a by-product, he is also entering his roses in the Chelsea Flower Show.

Monday 5th August

A big boost today for the White Ears Day. One of the major television companies is going to broadcast live from the palace and instead of being a one day event, it is now going to last a whole week. Mother has also clinched a deal to provide bed and breakfast for all of the television staff.

Tuesday 6th August

It now seems even more certain that a lot of money will be raised from the campaign, especially as Terry Wogan is away on holiday and will not be fronting the television coverage. I'm hoping I may be offered the job – it could lead to a whole new career.

Wednesday 7th August

Went for an interview today at the television studios. I got off to a bad start by arriving more than an hour late, although I did have a good reason. Mother told me to wear my best suit. It is not easy to decide which one is one's best when one has so many to choose from.

Thursday 8th August

I received a telephone call today to inform me I didn't get the job. It seems they wanted someone clean-living with a good image to host the show. They were obviously trying to get away from the royal family's current image. I think they'll probably go for Sir Cliff Richard and it'll make a change for him to be on television other than on Christmas Day, or Cliffmas Day as it is known in our household.

Friday 9th August

Only one day to go and everybody is really busy. As expected Sir Cliff is here and has been rehearsing but I had to laugh when he tripped over one of the corgis. I never thought he knew such language. Anne must have been giving him lessons.

Saturday 10th August

The big day is here at last. I just hope it is all worthwhile and that we raise enough money to keep us in the manor to which we have been accustomed. Mother has given me the very responsible job of standing outside the main gates selling the White Ears. I only had one person demand his money back because he said the ones being sold were not as big and hideous as the ones I had on. I pointed out I had not as yet put my White Ears on.

Sunday 11th August

Sir Cliff decided that as today was Sunday, it ought to be based on a religious theme. Mother agreed as she was always on the lookout for a chance to hand around the collection plate. Sir Cliff had the brain wave of our all celebrating Christmas early and hit upon the idea of selling mistletoe to bring in extra cash. It also gave him the chance to sing his songs, so it really was mistletoe and whine.

Monday 12th August

Many visitors came again today – the event is going very well. I heard it rumoured that even Mark Phillips came but nobody noticed him. Nothing much changes there then. Anne was sorry she didn't see him as she would have relished the opportunity to ignore him just like in the old days.

Tuesday 13th August

Today was put aside for organised coach parties to come. Womens' institutions ran coaches from all over the country, but theirs was not the biggest party to arrive. Ten coaches came from a club called 'Power'. It was only later I found out it stood for Princess of Wales Ex-Romeos. Still I managed to charge them twice – once on the way in and again on the way out. As they would have found out from Diana, we royals like to have it all ways.

Wednesday 14th August

More celebrities turn up here every day. Today Margaret Thatcher came and took her turn in going around with a collection tin. I think she may have an ulterior motive though. I'm convinced she still thinks that some day she'll take her rightful place as queen and then be entitled to her share of the money raised.

Thursday 15th August

Attendances dropped dramatically this afternoon. This seemed to coincide with the arrival of Bob Geldof, so I suggested to him he might like to do a concert in Philadelphia to raise money. Sure enough, as soon as he left the crowds flocked back.

Friday 16th August

Diana came today to do her bit. Although I think she was just making sure we were raising enough to ensure a decent amount for her divorce settlement. She seems determined to make sure she will be well provided for in the future. She even asked me if I'd make a will. I said no but I'd heard she had on several occasions.

Saturday 17th August

The last of a very successful week which should ensure that the monarchy will survive for many more years. We finished off with a grand fireworks display and let Sarah take charge of the sparklers. Even she couldn't lose those, and I took great pleasure in giving Diana a rocket.

Sunday 18th August

Anne has been in a terrible mood for the past few days and we've just realised why – we'd forgotten that last Thursday was her birthday. She said that nobody would even notice if she had died. I tried to pacify her and promised we would go out and get her something really special so she would know how much we cared about her.

Monday 19th August

I should have organised Anne's present myself but I let Father do it. I even told him what to buy but he still got it wrong. I told him that Anne would really like it if we all clubbed together and bought her a new horse. Imagine her horror when a brand-new hearse turned up at her door. Father had misheard me – Anne was mortified, so to speak.

Tuesday 20th August

William and Harry will soon be going back to school. I had rather a nasty shock today when Diana sent me the bill for their school fees amounting to £8,000 each per term. That works out at nearly £50,000 a year. I think I will write to the school to complain as it seems ever such a lot to pay when all the boys need to know is how to walk with their hands clasped behind their backs, how to read speeches written for them, and how to shake hands.

Wednesday 21st August

Mother was equally horrified when I told her about the school fees, although she did say that it could easily be paid if Diana were to cancel one of her many holidays each year. When I mentioned this to Diana she was not happy and told me to get away. She then disappeared.

Thursday 22nd August

The tricky problem of the school fees has now been solved with Father's help. He pointed out that as neither Diana nor myself were working or ever likely to, we would be entitled to send the bill off to the Social and get them to pay it.

Friday 23rd August

Had a nice surprise in the post today. Edward is to star in a new musical. Not only that but he has also been put in charge of costumes. He seems to be making quite a success out of his chosen career. He has sent the whole family tickets to next Tuesday's premiere.

Saturday 24th August

You'd have thought that Mother would have been proud that her youngest son was to play the leading role in a West End show, but she seemed more concerned that Edward had only got us front row seats and not the royal box. It turned out the Thatchers had got there first.

Sunday 25th August

The palace is still open to the public and we seem to be getting even more visitors now that Mother has decided to open the whole house. This can prove to be rather embarrassing especially if one happens to be on the throne. It is most off-putting to have a coachload of ladies gawping at your private quarters.

Monday 26th August

We are all looking forward to going to the theatre tomorrow.
Mother says we must all look our best for Edward's big day. She has
had me polishing her tiara for most of the day and she says we should
always be proud to show off the crown jewels.

Tuesday 27th August

What a shocker Edward's show was – it was a remake of the
musical *Hair*. I know Mother said that we should be proud to show off
the crown jewels but I do think that Edward took it a little bit too far.
I think he got a good deal though by being in charge of the costumes.

Wednesday 28th August

Edward came around today to see what we all thought of the show.
Mother was still under sedation so he couldn't see her. Anne hurt his
feelings by asking Edward how he managed to have the starring role
whilst having such a small part. Father said he thoroughly enjoyed it
but would rather have seen the dress rehearsal.

Thursday 29th August

Mother was feeling a little bit better today but she couldn't
understand why Edward would want to take part in that type of show.
I said it only goes to prove that you must be crazy to be an actor and
to appear on stage without any clothes on just shows you're nuts.

Friday 30th August

Camilla is planning to have a garden party on Sunday to which I
have been invited. I think she has arranged this so she can get some
practice in for when she becomes queen. She said Andrew, Anne and
Edward would also be very welcome to attend if they weren't busy. I
didn't know about Andrew or Anne but I knew that Edward didn't
have anything on so he wouldn't be able to come.

Saturday 31st August

Mother still hasn't fully recovered from the shock of Tuesday's performance yet. She won't speak to Edward let alone see him. She said she'd seen far too much of him recently and more to the point so had everybody else, seeing that photographs of the show had been published in the national newspapers in colour - royal blue.

Sunday 1st September

It was a beautiful day today - ideal conditions for the garden party. Camilla arranged everything. There was plenty of food and drink and she even arranged games for her guests. The highlight of the day for me was having Bowles on the lawn.

Monday 2nd September

Back to school today for William and Harry after their long summer break. It is a tradition that parents accompany their children on the first day back, so Diana and I went along with about five hundred other mothers and about a thousand fathers. I could never understand why there are always more fathers than mothers there, although I'm sure I glimpsed Will Carling and James Hewitt there as well.

Tuesday 3rd September

It is far quieter at home now. Although the palace is still open to the public there are far fewer visitors now that the children are back at school. I have even been able to go to our dining room without having to queue for my midday meal. Mother still insists that I pay the same rate as visitors for my lunch even though I usually have to do all of the washing and wiping up.

Wednesday 4th September

You can tell that autumn is now here as it gets quite chilly in the evenings. Father said if I want to keep warm, I should turn the boiler on but unfortunately Camilla has gone to stay with her parents for a few days.

Thursday 5th September

Mother has asked me to get the palace boilers serviced to ensure the heating will be working for the winter. I think I'll go straight to the gas board because I'm worried that if I get any corgi registered contractor, I could end up with a vet calling.

Friday 6th September

Now that the palace has been open to the public for a month, it is looking rather the worse for wear, so Mother has decided that tomorrow is to be the last day for this year at least. We have all been instructed we are to help out next week with major decorations.

Saturday 7th September

The last of the open days is over and what a state the place has been left in. The carpets are scuffed and worn – souvenir hunters have removed strips of wallpaper from the walls and Mother was most upset to find chewing gum stuck to the throne especially as she didn't see it before she sat down.

Sunday 8th September

I have had a very lazy day today as Mother said that from tomorrow we are going to be very busy sprucing up the palace. I did suggest to her that we ought to get professionals in to do the job but she said it would cost far too much. I have worked out that the cost of repairs and replacements will come to more than we took at the turnstiles. Prices will definitely have to go up next year and no one will be allowed in unless they bring their slippers.

Monday 9th September

I wish that Mother would explain herself clearly. I spent hours polishing the sword, ushered the Prime Minister into her room and she just looked at me totally bewildered. "Why have you brought Mr Major here?" she asked.

"Just following your instructions," I replied.

"What instructions?" she groaned.

"You said today we were going to have major decorations."

Tuesday 10th September

After yesterday's incident, Mother has instructed me to start removing the wallpaper. I tried to get out of it but she did not accept my argument that stripping was more in Edward's line of work.

Wednesday 11th September

Wallpaper stripping can be a slow and tedious job but at least today I had a willing helper. Father had been ordered to assist and he said he would be glad to do so. It's not often he gets the chance to tear Mother off a strip.

Thursday 12th September

Finished getting the wallpaper off in Father's room today and found that one of the walls was only half plastered. Mother said that usually the rooms show some of their occupants' characteristics, so she was therefore somewhat surprised to find the room wasn't completely plastered.

Friday 13th September

Diana came to see how the work was progressing. She certainly picks her moments as I was in the middle of painting the ceiling and some paint dripped off the brush onto her. She was most annoyed and shouted, "I don't know what I ever saw in you Charles." I told her to get out and not to return until she was feeling less emulsional.

Saturday 14th September

Fed up with the decorating, I decided to take the weekend off. I was just about to go out this afternoon when Mother said, "You can't go out yet, Prince, you've got paint on the crown."

"Don't be silly, Mother," I replied, "I wouldn't be stupid enough to wear the crown whilst decorating."

"Not that crown," she answered, "the crown that your hair used to grow from, son."

Sunday 15th September

William and Harry came to see me today because it is Harry's birthday. Knowing how keen he is on sport, I wanted to get him a present that would please him but annoy his mother. I managed to succeed well on both counts because I bought him a replica Welsh international rugby union kit.

Monday 16th September

Back to work today and I have been getting on quite well with the painting. The doors and skirting boards have got a nice shine to them now, which should please certain members of the press who recently stated the House of Windsor had lost a lot of its gloss in recent years.

Tuesday 17th September

After the painting I tried my hand at wallpapering today, and got on surprisingly well. It is amazing what you can cover with a few rolls of wallpaper. I don't somehow think that papering over the cracks will be as easy in the room I used to share with Diana.

Wednesday 18th September

One room successfully completed – only another five or six hundred left to do. I'm amazed when I hear that some families can completely redecorate their whole house in a matter of weeks. I suppose they must be large families with everybody pitching in to help.

Thursday 19th September

Now that I've got the decorating bug, I've decided to get straight on and do my room next as I want to remove all traces of Diana from the room. I took great pleasure in scraping off the Bambi wallpaper. Bambi's big sorrowful eyes always remind me of Diana's performance on *Panorama*.

Friday 20th September

I have finished removing the paper and spent the day painting. In order to save time I sent Andrew out shopping for new wallpaper as I thought I could trust him to come back with something suitable. I told him to get anything that wouldn't remind me of Diana.

Saturday 21st September

Andrew brought the wallpaper round today. First he gave me a roll of paper picturing rugby players – his idea of a joke. He then gave me the correct paper which he said he hoped would remind me of the happier days of my youth. It was designed by Enid Blyton and featured Noddy and Big Ears. I fail to see how Andrew could think of it as being appropriate.

Sunday 22nd September

I phoned Camilla today to let her know that I had finished the bedroom. She sounded quite excited and came straight over to inspect the work. She took one look and said, "You can get that lot off right now." I never thought she would be as thrilled as that and started to take off my trousers. "What on earth are you doing now?" she bellowed. "I was not referring to your clothes – I meant that ghastly wallpaper. I can see which character is you but I certainly don't like being portrayed as a funny looking chap in a floppy hat."

Monday 23rd September

I don't know what hurt the most. The fact that I was going to have to repaper the bedroom to keep Camilla happy or that she thought I resembled Big Ears. I think I may have to resort to plastic surgery... I must find out who Michael Jackson uses because I wouldn't like him to get his hands on me or I could end up the first black King of England.

Tuesday 24th September

I broached the subject of plastic surgery with Mother but she did not think it necessary and told me not to be such a dumbo. That convinced me... If I really do look like that cartoon elephant then drastic steps must be taken.

Wednesday 25th September

I have booked an appointment for tomorrow with one of the country's leading plastic surgeons. Camilla thinks I'm being silly and going to a lot of unnecessary expense. She said she would never waste money on plastic surgery. I retorted that she'd never be able to afford all the work that needs doing.

Thursday 26th September

I visited the surgeon and he seemed very encouraging once he had stopped laughing. He suggested he could pin back my ears on a temporary basis so that I could see what it looked like and whether it felt comfortable. I decided to go away and think about it and would let him know my decision.

Friday 27th September

Somehow the press got hold of the story that I had been to see the surgeon and they printed the story with the headline 'Prince's ears in a flap', which I did not appreciate at all. In fact it made me more determined to do something about it.

Saturday 28th September

Camilla visited today and could see I was upset about the newspaper article. I told her I couldn't understand how the papers had got hold of the story. She said that nothing can be kept from the press because walls have ears. I said I thought they only had ice cream, but if I found out who spread the story they'd not only have ice cream in their ears but in every other orifice as well.

Sunday 29th September

Camilla admitted today it was her who had leaked the story to the press because she was upset at the comments I'd made about her needing extensive plastic surgery. She only admitted it because she loves ice cream and couldn't wait for me to carry out my threat. She also made me promise to lick it all off afterwards, so I spent a most enjoyable evening setting about her with Mr Whippy.

Monday 30th September

I returned to the surgeon today after deciding to go ahead with the temporary alterations to my ears. Although it was painful, I hope it will be worth it as it cost a king's ransom. I don't yet know how it looks because I have to leave the bandages on for a couple of days.

Tuesday 1st October

Well, at least these bandages are providing great entertainment for the rest of the family. Andrew said that if William and Harry aren't sure who their father is, they will now be fortunate to have two mummies.

Wednesday 2nd October

These bandages are proving to be great as a disguise. I managed to go to central London and spend the whole day there without being recognised. They could also improve my job prospects as I was offered a job as a waiter in an Indian restaurant which I mistook for the job centre.

Thursday 3rd October

I took the bandages off today and was quite impressed with my new look. Camilla liked it too although she said my ears still stuck out a little bit. She thought I looked like a former England captain. I was livid until she explained she meant Gary Lineker – not Will Carling. She rather liked my crisp new image.

Friday 4th October

Even though all the comments about my ears were favourable, I decided to have the operation reversed, or should I say the decision was really made for me. As is my regular custom, once a week I put on the crown in order to get used to the feel of it. As soon as I put it on it slipped down over my ears because I no longer had anything to support it. There was no way I was going to sacrifice my chances of becoming king by improving my looks.

Saturday 5th October

I had further discussions with my surgeon today and he suggested there is an alternative. He could fit loops to my head behind each ear so I could wear earrings at the top of each ear that attached to the loops, pinning my ears back. I would then be free to unhook the loops whilst wearing the crown. It could set off a whole new fashion trend.

Sunday 6th October

Mother won't allow it. She says if I wear earrings she will never abdicate and I will remain Prince Charles for ever. I suppose I will have to be satisfied with the good looks I was born with.

Monday 7th October

Mother has called a big family meeting for this Wednesday. This is a most unusual occurrence and she is insisting that everybody attends. There surely can only be one reason for calling such an important meeting and that is to announce her long overdue retirement.

Tuesday 8th October

I'm getting really excited about tomorrow's meeting. I have been wearing the crown virtually all day today just to get used to the weight of it. Mother went out for the afternoon today and that gave me the chance to raid her wardrobe. The robes for special occasions really seem to suit me.

Wednesday 9th October

What a big let-down the meeting was – not even a mention was made of retirement! Mother did have a go at Edward though because she noticed that her wardrobe had been disturbed and she thought he had been trying on her dresses again. Although Edward denied it, I don't think Mother believed him. I'm sure she doesn't suspect me.

Thursday 10th October

The subject of yesterday's meeting was the New Year's honours list. Mother wants the existing system revamped so has asked all of us to come up with new ideas of how the scheme should work and who deserves awards. I think we should charge people who receive medals to generate much-needed income.

Friday 11th October

I have thought of the first award I would like to see given under the new scheme. I would like Will Carling made a Dame of the British Empire. I would ensure the award was given with a specially-made blunt sword and I would be delighted to officiate personally at the ceremony.

Saturday 12th October

Seeing as how I have decided to award Will Carling with a deserved honour, it seems only fair the lovely Diana should get one as well. As she is a special case she should get a brand new award, so I have replaced the CBE with the new BSE – an award the mad cow so thoroughly deserves.

76

Sunday 13th October

I have noticed that in previous years there have been many awards made to the entertainment industry. I think there should be a new category just for entertainers for I am sure this idea would be very popular with Edward as he could nominate his actor friends for awards.

Monday 14th October

Tomorrow is Sarah's birthday. I never mind buying her a present because she usually puts it to good use. For instance, I remember when she was expecting her first baby. As a joke, I bought her a book entitled – *Ridiculous Names for Children*. I was forgetting that she doesn't have a sense of humour and she has now used the book twice.

Tuesday 15th October

I managed to get the ideal present for Sarah but I don't know if she will appreciate it. I wanted to get something she would find useful so I bought her a baby's dummy. If it can stop a baby from sucking its fingers it may stop her from sucking someone else's toes.

Wednesday 16th October

Back to the serious business of the New Year's honours awards. The awards for entertainers could be on similar lines to the Oscars only it would be apt if they were named after Edward. Perhaps we should call them the Teddies and they could be presented at the annual Teddy ceremony.

Thursday 17th October

Another thought struck me today – we could save money on the entertainers awards by not giving the recipients medals. Instead they could be presented with Teddy Bears! On second thoughts, after Edward's recent starring role in *Hair*, this should be changed to Teddy Bares.

Friday 18th October

If Mother likes my fabulous idea about the Teddy awards, I think it is only fair that I have an award named after me, although I don't want my awards to be a copy of any other. I want the recipients to be proud to own an original proper Charlie.

Saturday 19th October

William and Harry start their half term holiday today so they are going to stay with me for the first half of the week, and spend the second half with Diana. It almost feels like I am taking part in a rugby match and being substituted at half-time. I bet I can guess who I'll be replaced by.

Sunday 20th October

The boys have been telling me about how they are getting on at school. Last week they had a special careers week which entailed speakers coming into the school to give talks on various career opportunities. William felt this was a total waste of time as not one king was invited to speak to or advise the boys.

Monday 21st October

William said that, like him, many of his friends at school are expected to go into the family business when they leave, and in preparation their proud parents have already amended the name of their firms to read for instance – Smith and Son, or Jones and Son. William can't understand why I'm not included on Mother's headed notepaper as Queen and Son, rulers of distinction. Sounds good to me!

Tuesday 22nd October

I had a chat to William about his future career. I gave him my considered fatherly advice which was not to worry about what his teachers said as I have got his life fully mapped out. For the next fifty years he will take if easy and do nothing, and after that he will be king. It is really the opposite to ordinary people as he and I get our retirement first and then start work later.

Wednesday 23rd October

Harry's future career will be completely different from William's as he will almost certainly never become king. I have been encouraging Harry to study hard to get all the qualifications he can as he is a bright lad. I have great hopes that he will take up a career which will be of use to the family. I thought he might like to work in the legal profession, perhaps as a divorce lawyer.

Thursday 24th October

The boys have gone to spend the rest of their holiday with their mother. She has very kindly managed to arrange to have a few days with them in between holidays and boyfriends. If only Diana could have found three or four days every six weeks to have spent with me, then we might still be together.

Friday 25th October

Diana phoned today angry that I suggested Harry should go into the legal profession. She said she wants him to be a leading sportsman and if anyone from the family was to go soliciting, it would be her who would do it.

Saturday 26th October

What a lovely surprise I had today. William and Harry came back to stay with me again. Even better than that, Diana came round and pleaded with me to look after them as an emergency had arisen which she had to attend to – it was great to see her beg.

Sunday 27th October

I'm absolutely fuming as I found out from William what Diana's so-called emergency was. William said that Sarah visited them and had just booked two tickets for a holiday on the Virgin Islands which had been a cancellation. I'm even surprised the Virgin Islands would let them in.

Monday 28th October

I'm glad I'm not a full-time parent. I had to get up at six o'clock this morning to get the boys ready for school and then take them there. That's a full five hours earlier than I normally get up. I'm glad they don't go to ordinary day school as I couldn't face getting up that early every morning.

Tuesday 29th October

Mother called another meeting today to discuss our suggestions for the New Year's honours. By discussion I mean she told us she didn't like our ideas and there was no way she was going to hand out Teddies or Charlies and she certainly wouldn't even consider naming an award after William.

Wednesday 30th October

Diana and Sarah have already returned from their holiday which unfortunately for them had to be cut short. The brochure had said the hotel would treat all their guests like royalty but it turned out to be nothing like that at all. The hotel even expected them to pay for things they had.

Thursday 31st October

I've just received the hotel bill from Diana and Sarah's holiday which they very kindly arranged to be forwarded to me. Sarah was going to sell some of their jewellery so they could settle the bill but she had lost it at the airport, along with her credit cards I assume.

Friday 1st November

I've only just heard the news that Andrew and Sarah are divorced and it happened over six months ago. The rest of the family had been keeping it from me because of the trauma my marriage was causing me. It seems all the royal marriages except Mother and Father's are falling apart. I suppose that says something for separate bedrooms.

Saturday 2nd November

Thinking back, I am amazed that I didn't realise about Sarah and Andrew as they were even divorced when we went on our camping holiday. Now I understand why they were so keen on boys in one tent and girls in another. Even Camilla didn't twig, or if she knew, she didn't mention it to me.

Sunday 3rd November

Father nearly let it slip some months ago when he told me that Andrew and Sarah had managed a quickie, but I misunderstood thinking he was talking about something else. I feel awful about that now because I even congratulated Andrew on it.

Monday 4th November

I questioned Camilla today about whether she knew about Andrew and Sarah's divorce. It seems she knew all about it but decided not to tell me in case I got upset because Andrew has succeeded but I have not as yet. Anyway, she said she didn't want it widely known if it made me decide to have a quickie with Diana.

Tuesday 5th November

I am giving serious thoughts as to whether I should get rid of Camilla. It would certainly be cheaper to dump her now rather than after we were married. Another alternative is not to marry her but just to live together. She could then be my royal-law wife. (Mother wouldn't let me have a common-law wife.)

Wednesday 6th November

I'm still wondering if Camilla would make a suitable queen. I've got my doubts because like Diana, Camilla has no experience of royal life. I wonder if her hands could cope with all the constant hand shakes and if her eyes could stand the constant flashing – no, not from me, but from the gentlemen of the press.

Thursday 7th November

Only a week away from my birthday and I'm already getting excited. Mother has promised me a special day and said I mustn't make any arrangements as she has already organised something for me. I wonder if it's a coronation that she's got planned.

Friday 8th November

If I am to be crowned next week I should be giving serious consideration to the position of queen. Should I be looking for someone with royal experience? If so, Sarah is available, and she's not bad looking either, especially if you compare her with Camilla. She's already got a wedding dress as well, so it could be a cheap do.

Saturday 9th November

Well, I did it! I took the plunge and gave Sarah a ring. No, not an engagement ring, just a call on the telephone to see if she was busy for the next couple of weeks. She said she wasn't but was curious as to why I was asking. I just told her there might be an engagement coming up and she might be invited.

Sunday 10th November

If I did marry Sarah, I would be married to my ex-sister-in-law and be stepfather to my nieces. It would be very confusing for the girls as they wouldn't know whether to address me as Father or Uncle Charles – maybe they'd stick with the usual old 'Big Ears.'

Monday 11th November

I don't know if I fancy being father to two girls named Beatrice and Eugene because as the years pass and Sarah's previous marriage is forgotten, would I be blamed for their stupid names? Perhaps I should get their names changed to Elizabeth and Margaret to please Mother.

Tuesday 12th November

If I were to take on the role of father to somebody else's children I would expect them to change their surname to mine. I wonder how much it would cost me to change their names from Windsor to Windsor, and would anyone realise that I had taken the trouble to make the girls my own.

Wednesday 13th November

Only one day to go, who knows what tomorrow might bring. King Charles III sounds rather good doesn't it – unless of course you have difficulty in sounding your aitches. How am I going to break it to Camilla that I don't think she would make a good queen? I don't think I'll tell her until after tomorrow as I want to make sure I get my birthday present.

Thursday 14th November

Camilla got me up this morning. I might be another year older but I'm still not past it yet! Mother said she wasn't going to tell me what she had arranged for me until much later in the day. She told me to wear my best suit and to be outside Westminster Abbey at 7 p.m. tonight. This is it, I thought. Wrong! At 7 p.m. sharp I was met outside the abbey by Camilla. Mother had given her two tickets to the Royal Variety Show at a theatre around the corner. What a surprise! At least she was letting us have the royal box to ourselves. The Royal Variety Performance – a three hour show that seems to last a lifetime. The only royal engagement that nobody wants to attend and I get it as my birthday present. I wouldn't even give tickets to my worst enemy. Diana, yes – my worst enemy, no!

Friday 15th November

At least if I'm not to become king yet, I can hang on to Camilla for the time being. I'm glad I didn't ditch her the other day. She bought me an unusual present for my birthday saying it was to make me look youthful. It was a toupee or as she put it – a heirpiece.

Saturday 16th November

I've been feeling rather depressed for the last couple of days, ever since the Royal Variety Performance in fact. So I went to see the royal physician today who said he was expecting me yesterday. I said I wasn't aware I had made an appointment for yesterday. He said I hadn't but Mother always had to go to him the day after the show.

Sunday 17th November

Mother laid on a belated birthday tea for me today. I think she was feeling guilty for inflicting the show on me. She invited all the family except of course Diana. William brought me a crown that he'd made for me at school, but he made me promise to let him have it when I had finished with it. I told him the crown would naturally come to him. I think he's trying to get my job even before I've got it.

Monday 18th November

With each passing birthday, I wonder more and more if I will ever get the chance to rule the country. Realistically, Mother could continue to be monarch for another twenty years, by which time I would be already drawing my pension and well into my third or fourth marriage.

Tuesday 19th November

It's Mother and Father's wedding anniversary today and when I asked them what they wanted for a present they both said they would like a few days away in a top-class hotel. I managed to arrange it for them – Mother at a hotel in Edinburgh and Father in one at Eastbourne. I thought as they have separate rooms at home, it would make an ideal gift.

Wednesday 20th November

Now that Mother and Father have gone, I've taken the opportunity to move Camilla in temporarily. She has moved into Mother's room and seems to like it, especially the king-sized bed. She also says she gets an added thrill because there is a fair chance that an intruder will get into her room during the night.

Thursday 21st November

I took Camilla's hint and crept into her room in the early hours of this morning. She pressed the alarm button instinctively and I was dragged away by half a dozen security guards without Camilla even realising it was me. I spent three unpleasant hours being interviewed by detectives convinced I had broken into the palace by impersonating myself.

Friday 22nd November

I finally got released today after Camilla convinced the guards I was Prince Charles. She did it by making me strip off and show them the scars on my back where I had been continually stabbed by Diana. This, and the fact they couldn't remove what they thought were false ears, did the trick.

Saturday 23rd November

It is quite nice having Camilla stay here with me. She has been helping out with the household chores which relieves me of some of the responsibility. She is fond of animals and has even remembered to feed the remaining corgis. She also thought of keeping the dogs on the lead whilst taking them for a walk in the back garden. Last time I let them out it took three days to find them again.

Sunday 24th November

Mother and Father are due back tomorrow so I intended to make today special for myself and Camilla. However, nothing ever seems to go as planned and Camilla disappeared about midday, after breakfast, and I haven't seen her since. I ended up having a lovely romantic dinner for one.

Monday 25th November

Spent this morning tidying the house ready for my parents' return. Removed all traces of Camilla from Mother's bedroom. After lunch, as it was a nice day, I went for a stroll in the garden. After about half an hour I heard a sobbing sound and then traced the sobs to Camilla who had managed to get herself and the corgis lost in the garden. Still, at least they were still on their leads.

Tuesday 26th November

Mother and Father have both returned so things are pretty well back to normal. I had to confess to Mother that Camilla had used her room. Although I cleaned the room thoroughly, I didn't think to look under the bed and when Mother found a half-full chamber pot she guessed that someone had been there.

Wednesday 27th November

Mother brought me back a haggis from her holiday. She seemed very proud of it so I asked if she had shot it herself. She said she didn't but she did go into the shop and buy it herself – the first time she has gone shopping for many years.

Thursday 28th November

I had a chat with Andrew today. He seemed a bit low and said he had been feeling quite lonely since Sarah had gone. I suggested he ought to get out more and meet people, the only way to get a new girlfriend. Then I had a brain wave. Why didn't we both join the rugby club then we'd both get a chance of meeting someone, maybe even a princess.

Friday 29th November

Andrew did as suggested and applied for rugby club membership. He received a very short, curt telephone response stating the club had a very strict vetting procedure and his application had been rejected by the membership secretary, a certain Ms D. Windsor.

Saturday 30th November

St Andrew's Day. Mother is always very strict about these special days and insists that all of the menfolk wear kilts. I can never understand why, with the onset of winter, I have to wander around in a short skirt. They're right when they say it gets chilly around the Trossachs.

Sunday 1st December

I don't think I'll ever get warm again after yesterday. There are parts of me that turned blue, and Mother said it's only because of the blue blood running through my veins. I've even had a hot water bottle down the back of my trousers which became a bit embarrassing when I sat on the bed – it burst, forcing me to explain away the wet bed.

Monday 2nd December

Now that we are into December thoughts turn towards Christmas. Mother is getting worried about her annual Christmas Day broadcast to the nation. I've told her not to worry about it as people only watch it as they are too lazy to get up and switch the television off after watching *Top of the Pops*.

Tuesday 3rd December

Mother has been fretting about her broadcast all day today. She says the royal family seem to have been involved in scandals throughout the year and she certainly doesn't want to talk about that. I told her not to worry as I would write her speech for her. Anyway, it would be good practice for me as I hope to be writing them for myself from next year onwards.

Wednesday 4th December

The Christmas broadcast speech came quite easily to me. I decided to concentrate on all the good things that had happened during the year. I think the public would like to know about all of the money they had been saved – not just this year but for many years to come. This has all been due to the expulsion of Diana and Sarah from the family. Their extravagant lifestyles will no longer be financed by the civil list, saving millions.

Thursday 5th December

Now the speech is out of the way, I must start thinking about my Christmas shopping, which is another thing to be grateful for as my list won't be as long this year. I don't suppose I will get a card from Sarah this year now she has to pay for her own postage.

Friday 6th December

Aunt Margaret is always easy to buy for as she's happy to get the same present every year – a bottle of gin and a packet of cigars. We usually give her the gin when she arrives but leave the cigars until she is leaving the building, just in case.

Saturday 7th December

Now the boys are growing up, they won't want to be given toys any more. I think I'll get them some CDs. Maybe *Take That*'s greatest hits just to remind them of Diana and myself seeing as *Take That* split for good this year as well. I remember only too well some of Diana's greatest hits and I've got the marks to prove it.

Sunday 8th December

I've decided to really splash out on a joint present for Mother and Father this year. I have managed to book them in for a round-the-world cruise which visits almost every destination imaginable. The only thing is, it's due to last five years which means she will need somebody to replace her for at least the period she is away.

Monday 9th December

Edward has just told Mother he won't be able to attend our family gathering this Christmas as he has other commitments. He is doing well in his acting career and is booked to appear in pantomime for the next three months. Apart from Mother, that is probably the longest that any member of the family has been in work.

Tuesday 10th December

I've just heard that Edward is to appear in the pantomime *Palace in Wonderland*. It is said to be based on a true family story, where a king and queen get married and have many little princes and princesses who all marry in turn, but none of them live happily ever after.

Wednesday 11th December

Mother is not too happy about Edward's new role, as she thinks it may turn the royal family into a laughing-stock. Edward convinced her that his pantomime will not alter the public's opinion of us at all and she has now relented. Not only will she let him star in the show but she has also lent him a few of her best frocks.

Thursday 12th December

Edward very kindly got in touch today because he said he was short of somebody to play the part of the white rabbit in the show. But then he realised I wouldn't be suitable as I'm not a rabbit, only an heir. I did make a couple of suggestions if he was short of ugly sisters though – (ex-wife and future wife).

Friday 13th December

I wanted to start sending out my Christmas cards today but somehow I don't think my cards will be as good this year. A couple of years ago, I got Lord Snowdon to take a family photo of myself, Diana and the boys so that we could use them for Christmas cards. I've still got a lot of them left so, rather than waste them, I've cut Diana out and sent them off.

Saturday 14th December

Every year we always have a carol service especially for the royal family. Unfortunately the invitations went out to the same guests as last year which meant that Diana and Sarah were invited in error. Mother thought I might feel upset at Diana's attendance so she warned me in advance.

Sunday 15th December

Our local vicar got in touch today wanting to know which carols we require at our service. I suggested one especially for Diana's benefit – 'Oh Come All Ye Unfaithful.' I also said the collection taken at the service should be in aid of one-parent families.

Monday 16th December

Anne visited this evening – not a social call but on the scrounge again for one of her charities and we gladly donated some cash to her. It was well worth it just to stop her from damaging our ear drums with her carol singing. I remember when Anne and Mark used to go carol singing together, we used to nickname them Foggy and Foghorn.

Tuesday 17th December

William and Harry have just finished school for the Christmas holidays and they are getting very excited about what Father Christmas might bring them. I told them they were getting a bit old now to believe in Father Christmas so I wouldn't be dressing up for them this year. They said they always knew it was me because I could never get the hat over my ears.

Wednesday 18th December

I am struggling to think of ideas for the family's Christmas presents so I asked Mother and Father if they had any ideas. Mother said they were going to buy Anne a pony, so I decided to get her a tin of throat sweets – just the thing for when she gets a little horse.

Thursday 19th December

The Christmas tree arrived today and William and Harry enjoyed decorating it. They spent the whole day assisted by Father and Mother who said she really enjoyed herself and wished she could spend more time with her grandchildren. I said that could easily be arranged once she retired.

Friday 20th December

Only five days to go and I still haven't got Camilla a present yet. If is very difficult to know what to get her as she has got her heart set on an engagement ring, but I think it is too soon for that. I think I might pamper her by getting her a course of beauty treatment – that would benefit both of us. She would feel good and I'd be able to kiss her with my eyes open.

Saturday 21st December

I only have Edward's present to get now as I managed to get Andrew's present today. Andrew has been lonely on his own lately so I thought that getting him a pet would give him some company. Mother said that tact has never been my strong point but I should have been more thoughtful than to buy him a budgie.

Sunday 22nd December

The last present has been bought today which is a great relief. I have managed to get Edward a couple of dresses which Camilla helped choose. They are not for his acting career. I didn't want to get him clothes for work but I've heard he has an interesting social life.

Monday 23rd December

We had the annual carol service today. Diana and Sarah did attend and fully played their part in the nativity play – both as black sheep. Diana unexpectedly gave me a Christmas card enclosed with which were several of her bank paying-in slips.

Tuesday 24th December

Traditionally Christmas Eve is when the royal family open their presents. This is a tradition which was started by Father many years ago, because on Christmas Day he was always too drunk to get any pleasure out of it. The boys brought me a new polo shirt. It wasn't supposed to be a polo shirt but they had it too close to the fire and it burned a hole right through the middle.

Wednesday 25th December

After opening the presents the night before, Christmas Day always seems a bit of an anti-climax. We had a traditional Christmas dinner with Aunt Margaret setting fire to the Christmas pudding, which set Mother off in a panic, and it was inedible after she had hosed it down with the fire extinguisher. The highlight of the day was the compulsory viewing of Mother's Christmas broadcast. Next year it could be me.

Tuesday 26th December

Boxing Day is always the start of the great cold turkey festival which looks like it could last well into June next year. I blame Andrew for that as he always likes a big bird. By the look of it, though, this turkey could well outlast Sarah.

Friday 27th December

Mother and Father were very grateful for the tickets for the five-year cruise but unfortunately Mother has declined as she would have had to share a room with Father – something they haven't done since their honeymoon. She seems to be encouraging Father to go on his own though, and if he does, Mother says she will have to keep her job on to stop her getting bored. Another plan backfired, I fear.

Saturday 28th December

I'm getting a bit worried about William lately. He seems to be growing up very quickly and it won't be long until he's old enough to leave school. He seems to be getting very attached to Mother and what's more she is very fond of him. Perhaps I'm getting a bit paranoid but recently I have noticed Mother curtsying to him every time he enters the room.

Sunday 29th December

Just to be on the safe side, I've made enquiries about William joining the navy. All I've got to do now is somehow get him to sign his name on the bottom of the form and that would safely keep him out of the way for the next twenty years or so.

Monday 30th December

William came to me today as he is very concerned about his mother. Diana has got an obsession about her weight again and is going on to a strict diet. She told William she intends to lose two stone of useless fat over the next couple of months. I told him to send her to me and I'd help her to lose it in two seconds flat. I'd have her beheaded.

Tuesday 31st December

Last day of the year and it has ended as it began – no wife and no job. Still now is the time to look forward. I wonder what next year will bring. I think I will make two new year resolutions.

1. To become king.
2. To keep out of the newspapers as much as possible.